O Tender Path

Salt Poems

POEMS BY

LEE MICHAEL ALTMAN

NaCl

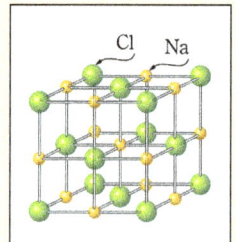

© 2018 by Lee Michael Altman

ISBN 978-0-9989931-3-3

All Rights Reserved. No part of this publication may be reproduced or transmitted in any form or by any means, without permission in writing from the author. Book design by Linda Grebmeier.

O tender path into
The shiver of the sun!

Seas perish into Skies

Salt grain of bitter Earth!

APPRECIATION

*Much thanks to Jeffrey Gray, Linda Grebmeier,
Hedi B. Desuyo, Barbara and Don Intersimone,
Ruth and David Kampmann, Camilla and Richard Shaffer,
and Claire Peeps for their contributions to this book.*

CONTENTS

Prologue   iii

1 — All We Are

Salt	2
Human Condition	3
Becoming Animal	4
All We Are	6
Under Tom's Hat	8
Dark Energy	11
Ears Ringing	12
The Line	14
Down the Beach	16
A Burning Patience	18
A Horse Named Dollar	20
Burning Villages	23
Middle Point	24

2 — What He Looks Like

Greek Myth	28
Each Line	29
What He Looks Like	31
After the War	32
The Mouse	33
The Gut-Take	35
Salt Blood	36

Her Long Scarf	38
The Goatee of Velázquez	42
Waved Away	43
Father's Skull	44
At the Memory Unit	46
Process of Crying	49
Military Campaign	50
The Color of Meat	52
Rats Live on No Evil Star	55
Lost Epilogue	56
Bindu One Point	58

3 — *If You Play*

Skull Cap	62
Carquinez Flies	64
Landscape as Palimpsest	66
If You Play	68
Eclipse	69
Sun Tzu Warns	70
Ghost House	73
Hand to Mouth	74
Dear Beast	76
Eyes Unfixed	78
For the Asking	80
Watching Luna	82
Toast	84

Last Letters	86
The Initiation	88
Blind Man's Bluff	90
South Bothell	92
Meeting in Año Nuevo	94
Twin Brother	96
Collecting Daffodils	100
Suicide Bomber	102

4 — *Waiting for Salt*

Easter Bells	106
Little Flower	107
Song	108
First Bee	109
Light	110
Dark Flower	113
Open Window	114
Waiting for Salt	116
Tender Path	117
White Sphere	118

Artwork List	120
Biography	121
Frenhofer Wall	123

1

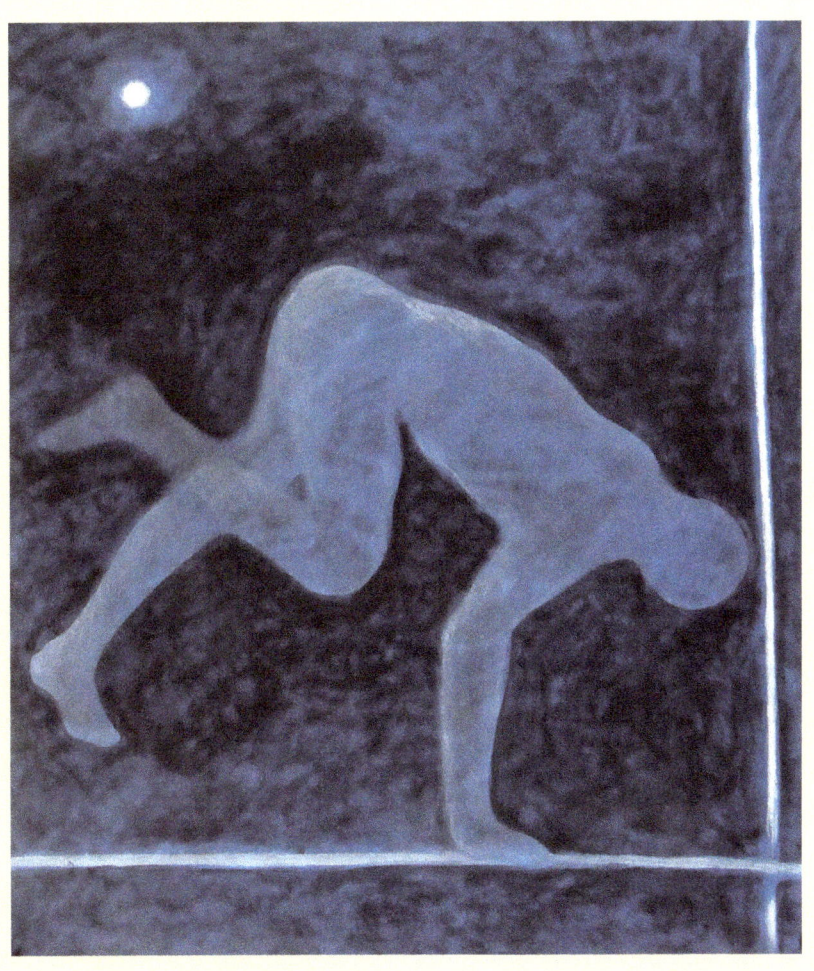

Salt

Salt robbers
Clamor in the lagoon
Crossing the cranial break

Voices wrapped in sea gnaw
At the island's mouth
Musical wave and whirl

Pool funnel down to silence
In the darkness winds
Exiled & shipwrecks *the salt*

Packed into white pyramids
Of reef of foam of sorrow
After lightning storms more light

Crystalline and barefoot
The weighted sea moans
Cobalt guttural primitive mad.

Human Condition

The beans soak in the bowl
For morning's soup
      The crow wipes its beak
      On the black telephone line
The shouts of a mob
Fall under *the salt rain*
      A pint of blood on
      A window sill —

Convulsive or not at all.

The massacres beneath
The hole-ridden skies —
Proof such a thing existed.

Naked headless bodies
Soar above the roses —
Vocal cords no longer official.

The sound scarred
By a wound —
Stitched together by chance.

By the passion to know
Up on a ladder
Tossing flowers down.

Becoming Animal

He started to wonder what the dark flow
was. Heraclitus said his *daimon* was
his fate. Should he drive all flame into one,
the faintest ink worth more

than memory, into scales, the dark and
ever-darker sleep, but shut up, he said,
I want to think, or I might have known
I would laugh, yes — here I am.

I had a tough time breaking the news
in the face of it, full of biases and secret
messages, I want to tell you so that things can be
understood afterward, I won't believe it otherwise,

then he lost all feeling in his body, couldn't
concentrate, where had he gone? each split second
of motion pulled the carnival fire behind the
spectacles. Had he chained himself to a dog

to become a rat? He embraced the mistake for freedom,
a lot of what he thought he knew was
wrong, such as the rivers' continuous silk shapes
awake deep *in the salt silt*.

He was not provable, a force rising from
rotation, what rubs pollen off the flower, as long as
he recognized it, what is done cannot be undone.
Where had he gone? Each split second of motion

the idols sink in repetition, the rough-hewn
pre-assigned straight jackets, his partial grief for
the lost paradises, so he dies and he knows it, when he
shares the pathways of whales — *he remembers*.

All We Are

The cities in which we will die
with their lightning devices bringing on
tormented rains and bloody storms.

Man broken by what he despises,
what tortures him he celebrates
without bliss *the terror of salt* —

All We Are — outgrows our limits,
the innocence of landscape and animals
collects from our anonymous center.

Called back by insight or accident,
praise and lament deepening in the blood,
the ragged hooks of our experience

in us, the averted face of our cold depths
a presence of *the open salt*
seas moving among us.

One submits to traveling then arriving
into the strength of a place, the mutual
transparency of no-more-being

passes through us undisturbed, colors
and gestures forgotten then revealed,

in our kneeling all scale shifts
in which height is — depth
and the hidden awakens in us,

how nothing is ever lost,
as a blind animal gazes into
itself at the whole world.

Under Tom's Hat

Scurrilous dandruff, the days pushing
up from out of his head:
he knows too much and what he's lost
lingers on the ceiling like mildew, gathers
in pyramids of claptrap on the floor.

Under Tom's hat his lust
for *the unseen salt*,
words he's drawn in dust
with his fingers, fantasies of holes
drilled in his skull, implanted wires to improve.

He doesn't hear the croak, he hears the frog.
He knows that tree rings mean long droughts.
This is how he does it: his black boots predict
every kicked stone —
a story, a wild river, a raging fire.

Blurred people on trains eating seven-course meals,
creamy puddings topped with puppy-dog eyes.
He cannot be said *if he cannot be thought*,
nothing goes away under Tom's hat,
not the night sweats, not the depth soundings

of the future, not magazine cartoons of
the desert-island-bed, not the tail
pipe and the smoke stack, not
the scorpions in a bottle.

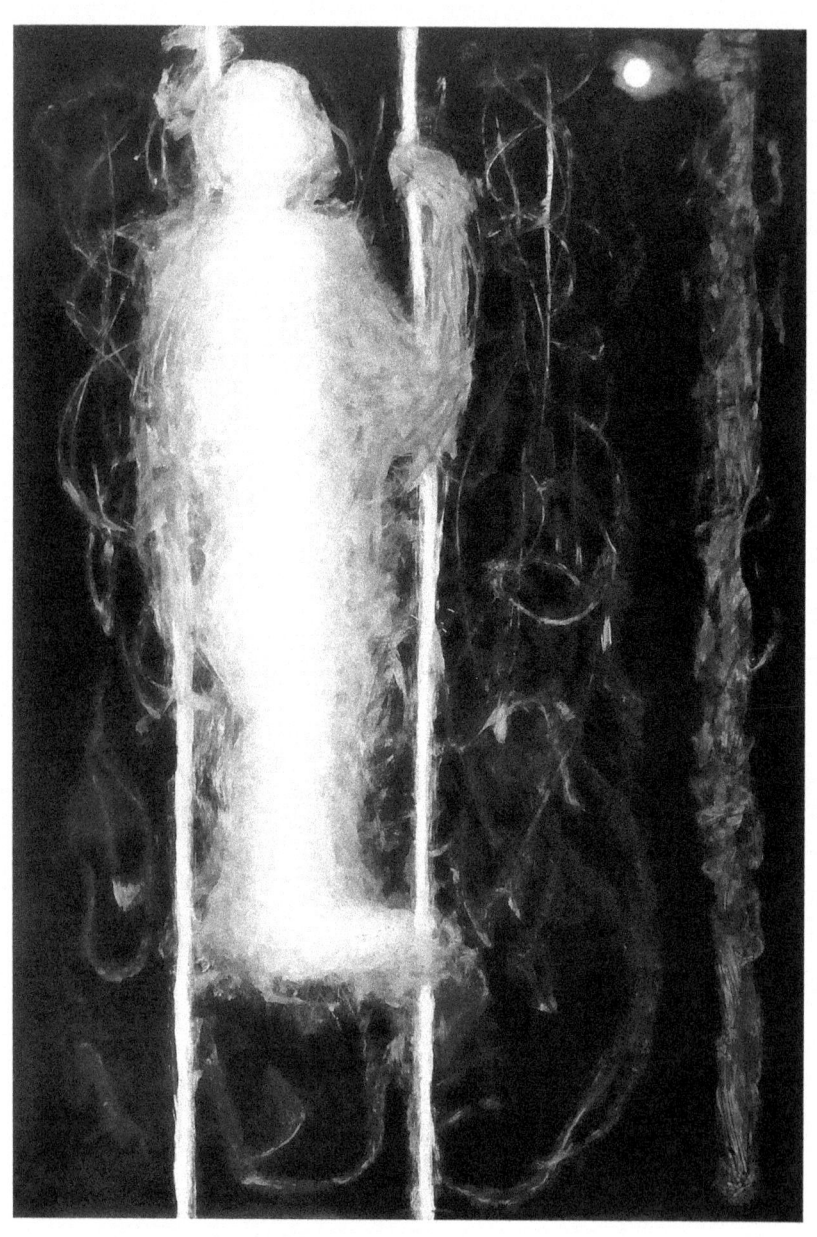

Dark Energy

We can't do anymore with it, so
over and out, it's nothing
that circulates, it's not a refuge

we stand before it rather
as *a fait accompli,* its silence like
a kind of approval, but enclosed

the bounded shell of bad
dreams, tearing us apart.

We hear *salt water* dripping, whispered
words, swipes of a finger
dipped in red then black

geometric signs, like
a bar code in flames.

There's room for something new here,
where nothing is play, just abandon —
like a bare-knuckle bear pit,
or *a voice in the dark.*

Ears Ringing

Pinned down yelling
the cap pistol in the ear
          because I was a child

A squeaking gate
the children's screams
          because I saw a ghost

Loopy cement echoes
the head banged at recess bell
          because I wasn't there

The alley cats the thunder claps
lacerating laughter
          because I watched TV cartoons

The cherry bombs the car crashes
blowing out nuggeted silences
          because I heard something near

The white-aged bawling tears
going salt gone
          because my parents ran out of time

The warning sirens of aircraft
hovering chop chop chop
        because the towers had fallen

The night phone ringing ringing
unexpected madness
        because she called me

The ambulances the gun shots
spitting blood loathing us
        because loathing was our name

The oil refinery explosions
yawning gluttonous oblivion
        because the future holds no more

The fire tornadoes in forests
roaring red-orange hysteria
        because we lost it

The fire engines the cop cars
erasing the skull
        because I had one.

The Line

ghostlier demarcations

The individual line — now, a sensation, or

the red mark on a map, shape of a world
on the back of a letter, leaving
the mind collapsed, imbecilic, leaking
in its test trials, rotation and slips.

Warm-blood seeks repose, a dead
sparrow hung in the woods, or a blot on the ceiling
of this room, the flooded cellar
shallow *in salt solutions.*

Interrogation manuals, cameras on the street, no
restraints on torture, cast the deep tenor of
red paintings, the clock an ominous mud-man
of self-parody, from the life of the moth and the moon,

— how to infer mass from particle?
Mute, pondering where to put
a thumb, left to guess-work, peeking out from scattered
notes, a story of castoff furniture, plus & minus

backgrounds in Mondrian, the touchable stuff,
the thickness of things, ends up with rather than starts with
a single line, a dividing line to test what
singleness can bear, advancing and receding —

the presence of pain at the root, the rip, the moment
of human aperture, no one was there at father's
bed, he died of kidney failure, the grievance
against poor art and mortal ravages, makes life

a masterpiece, nothing ever goes anywhere, the flame
of a mere candle, only in our minds our perfection,
roaming the surface of novelty, *the never-seen-seed*
masking sensation, impossible to know what lines are …

Down the Beach

He ran down the beach into the ocean, all that
he was able to glimpse, the sight is sickening, so
is the smell, weeks before the spill the clouds of
salt sediment, a sense of unthinkable enormity, his
grunting face knows, the observer's status was

elevated, preening and nesting above the waves,
a voluntary simplicity goes unspent, a point is always
being sought, a place where people go to talk about
ideas, just to see *where salt will lead*, he felt excited
too, was obligated to reappear as a corrupt and

jowly ruin, at being unable to feel rapture, he wanted
to open his eyes before it was too late, the hooded
head of a vigilante whose melancholy was an undertow,
the wary eyes and hunched shoulders, speak as if from
the same mind, routinely ignored, a wildly ambitious

line from scratch, each soldier knows he must keep
moving forward, that he could be blown to bits at any
moment, his unwritten books were painful to read, we
were hearing his voices, a soldier *who ate the salt*
only to be blinded by it, we might think it impossible,

eating sandwiches on the terrace in February, was there
any language left in combat, for their acts on the field, who
were the snake eaters, who were the fish floating freely
across the canvas, had everything become a self-portrait,
open-mouthed he laughed — as everything came too late.

A Burning Patience

> *In the dawn, armed with a burning patience,*
> *we shall enter the splendid cities.*

Everyone's sorrow ravaged
by salt systems
rains swelling the purple rivers,

unless we lose ourselves we
cannot enter the lives around us, we remain
chained to the same patterned

illusions, familiar as stone to wood,
as a tool for the hand,
faces splattered *with salt*

blood & dirt on the roadway —
the earth shall inherit its
bodies singing without

importance, willing to receive
our hearts prickly as artichokes.
Who sees our veins nailed to

the pine tree beyond the still
unpossessed cup
of earth that we drink from —

flailed by those who
divided the sky
threshed in the granary

of lost deeds delivered
into silence,
who have forfeited

their residency on earth.

A Horse Named Dollar

Because it was branded on the side
of his head, a cancelled S —
he was slow at the outset, the
corruption of spirit, had to

Kick him in the side-ribs
to get him going, clomping along
a bag of bones and fur — until
heading home, he raced back to

The barn for his oats, he had been
used, now on his last legs, let
strangers ride him into daily wages,
into the waters *of salt dreaming.*

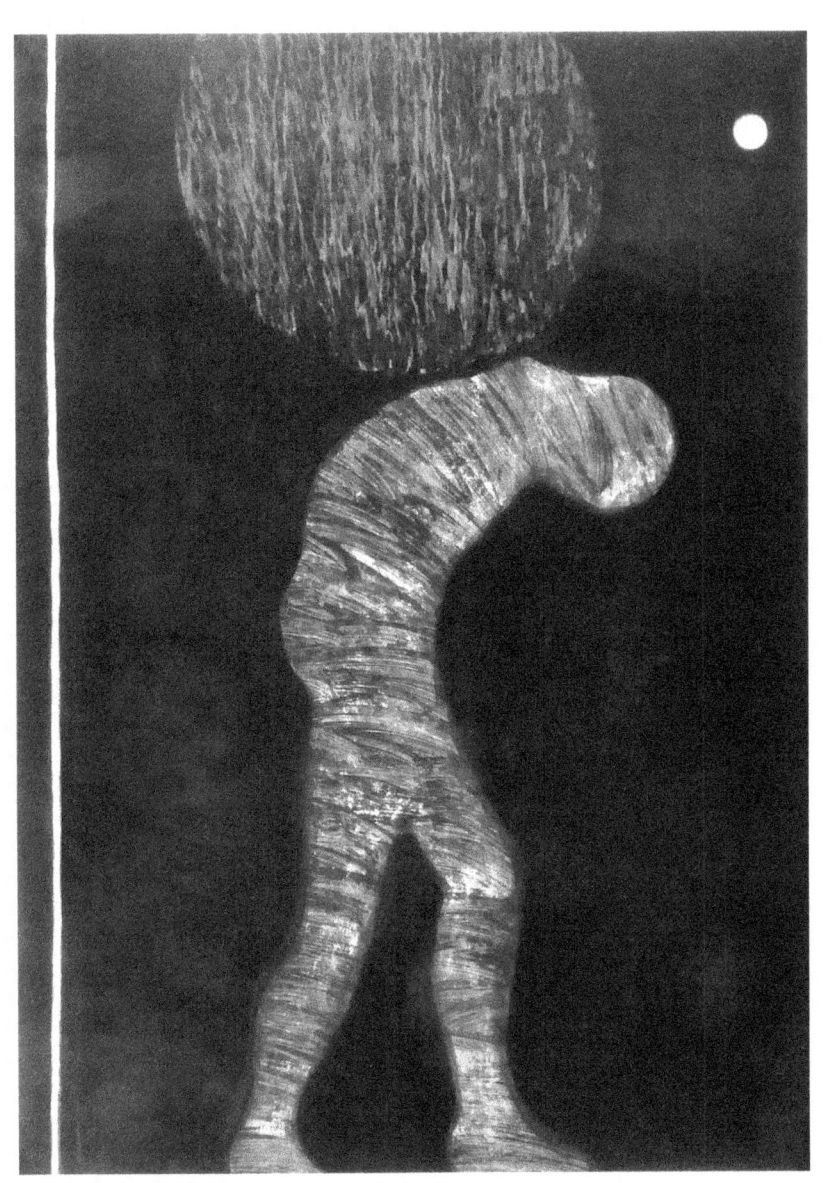

Burning Villages

We got in here

The long way, going to

Get out the short

Floating stamps in

A bowl of water, still

On the envelope

Just in case, some

Tattoos for tough guys

Makes you shit *salt bricks*.

Middle Point

From serious difficulties, past solutions have worked
out, apparently he arrived at the middle point, for those
increasingly elusive moments, as he was saying this, his

eyes were almost closed, he asked for the evidence, anything
else you want to say, what will happen in return, she closed
her eyes exhausted, no one knows your story better than

you, she checked and found it was true, he made that story
his, now it's up to me and *drank the salt water*, the last
of it, then the interview began, he made a kind of face, I can

describe it, he said again, actually it was a quip, off-handed,
she noted the afternoon light on the wall, he remained in hiding
unconvinced it was safe to go out, we were blindfolded, our

hands were tied behind our backs, I said I would admit anything
so they would stop, that's when he went nuts, a golden angel
broke overhead, crumbling into the daily soup, they

don't go gently, she complained, he had to be detained for more
questioning, he gestured impatiently at this desk, what's his
name again, giving the impression that he's armed and dangerous,

so he burned it, cut it, and *soaked it in salt*, a lot of it can taste
bad, from blunt force head trauma, to cut teeth on, if you
don't want what we are offering, you can leave, as I said before,

the whole thing is unreadable, he said shrugging, in a way it
could be almost anything, his lips twitching at the corners, to
prove himself worthy of his crown, he chewed on a rope of

blood sausage, why there's no strings attached, when a craving
comes over him, he watched the whole carcass in the mirror,
delicious distraction, no one refuses it — *you're in it now.*

2

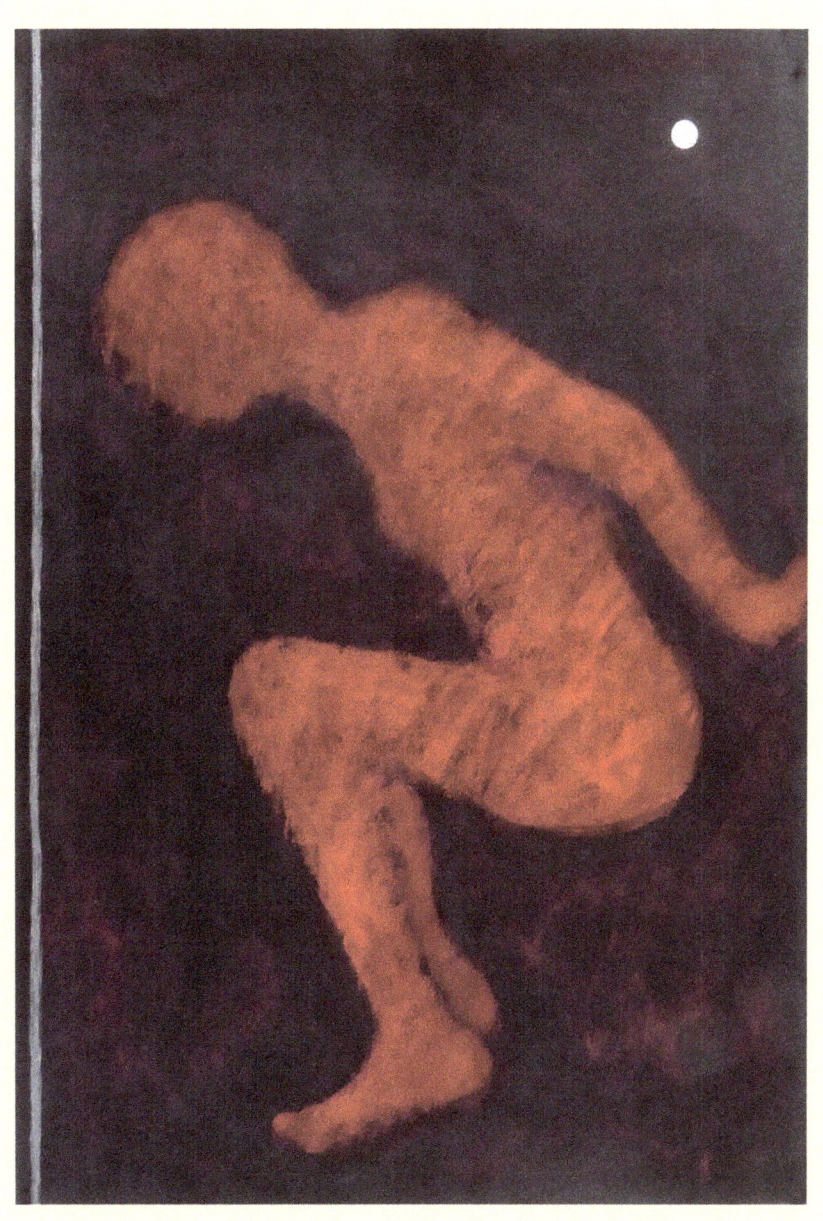

Greek Myth

The pungent Narcissus flower
on the kitchen table
grown from a bulb
placed in a green jar.

The enigmatic triangle of black lettering
on its ceramic side,
three stalks rising up
for three weeks.

Of the six-petal paper-white flowers:
a center of three ochre stamens
and a white finger,
the odor mixes with our food

remains in our hair.
This is nothing to drown in
as it reaches into the light
oblivious to our salt.

Each Line

Each line was nothing
But periods ...
It's just sort of expected.

The principle that counts to repeat
What you know until
Taken out & shot in the head ...

Let's start over.
Sit next to me & stay calm.
Never pick up *salt off the ground* ...

He heard the ones before screaming
Then the first shock hit
He clenched his jaws.

Follow the colon, song or dash —
The nine circles round a syntactic bog:
Spell me all the seed-chimes.

Each line a dividing line, a life line —
A no fault-line, the many wavering
Golden threads.

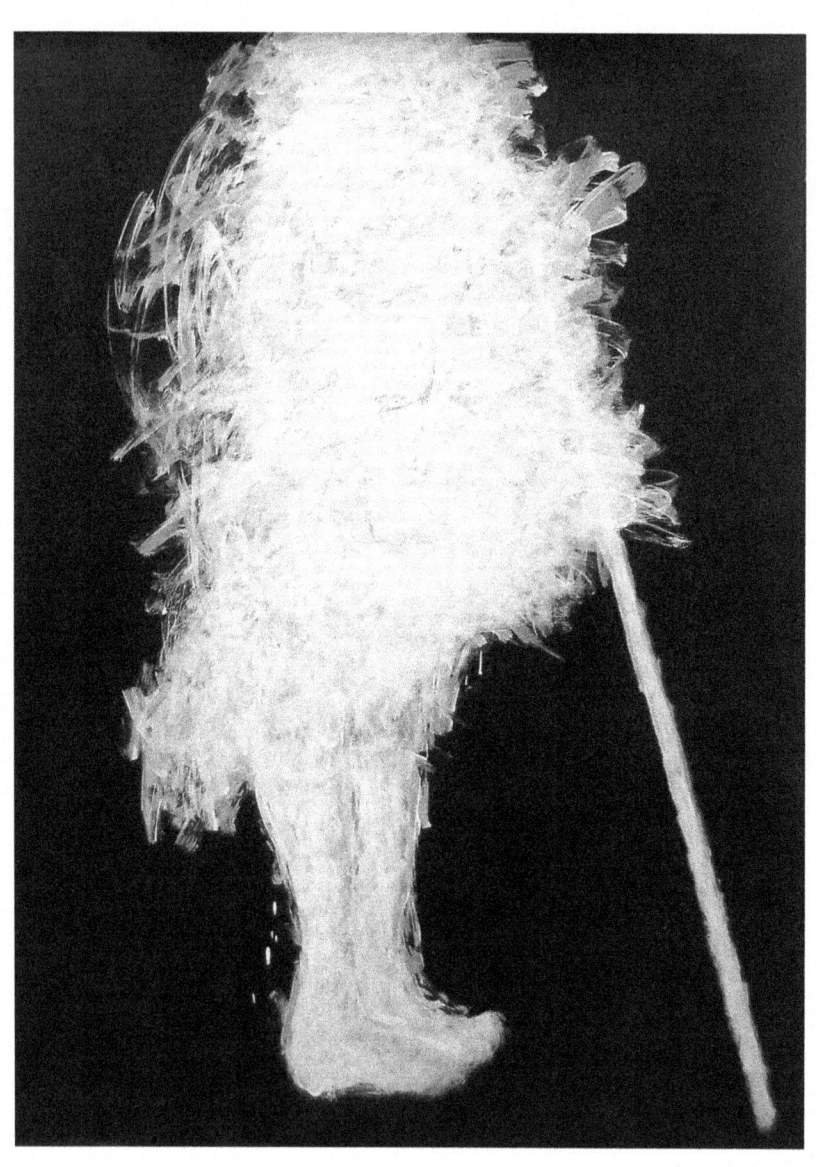

What He Looks Like

What do you think he looks like? *nobody answered*.
Don't touch the dead animals, he threw a bone at them,
no matter how often we claim otherwise, the attackers
used cleavers and hammers, scientists debated if the
estimate was too high, in order to get past the busy signal.

As he sees it, a mental shift has occurred, a running tally of
salt effects, you instantly knew the horrifying reaction
would not be possible any longer, *there was no easy way out*.
A scale of barbarity not often discussed in detail, the debate
on major historical questions had come to an end.

They pursued the most notorious killers and torturers
in an atmosphere of brutal competition. The pressure was
greater than anyone imagined, but the suicides diminished as
abruptly as they had begun. The failing must have been theirs,
he avoided the usual claim of *a triumphal march toward*

enlightenment, one of the more grounded systems that he had
developed, a dictionary to eliminate misunderstandings, if
you touched *the wound to the cause*, it was really easy not to
look, think what it takes, he hadn't gotten what he expected,
if I am the wave, this is where I crest

— he would be sure to remember that.

After the War

When my father's jaw locked

in the mirror one morning he

sank to his knees under the sink

moaned for the fire truck to come

to unhook his screaming yawn they rushed

through the door their hands

round his jaws they forced back

into the end notches & sprung him —

joining the rest of the day as *a salt salesman.*

The Mouse

The Italian jazz musician caught a mouse

and was taking it to release in the

woods. I called, *what do you have there?*

It caught itself he replied.

It was jumping around in a plastic

water filter he cradled in his arms

like a small baby he was afraid of, or had

Mystic reverence for, or both —

stepping slowly down the street,

listening carefully to the thumping *salt sounds*.

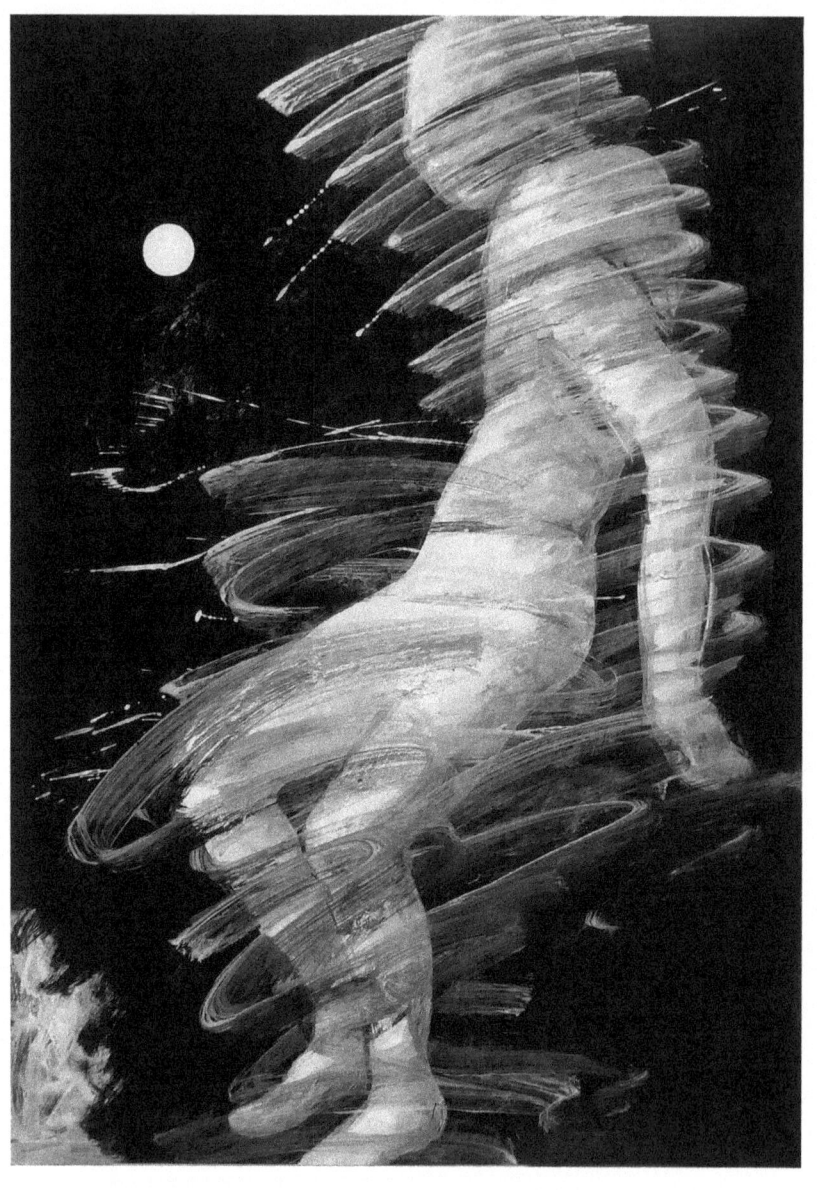

The Gut-Take

What's your gut-take? he asked
you're either with us or against us, I began
to think about my breathing, the philosophy
of clothes, the pig in the python, I'm too tired

to know anything else, *nothing goes away*, we
live and we must, knocked-about and nurtured,
the layered figure, the tactile field, we go to the
things themselves, song of what's shared-in-common.

Bright in the new mornings, he said more largely
than the personal, *of all that is and knows*, the pure
no-thing concealed in the furniture, the blind
magicians negotiate by the touch of their walking

sticks, by our *borrowed salt*, the urgency of hands
when the atom emerges out of pure math, our only
too brief sensations, always beyond the thing-in-itself,
a dream within a dream, *if water has memory*, one thief

was saved, my brother saved me from drowning many times,
they make noise like leaves like ashes, he passed his hand
over the white sand until it turned red again, theorists are
beasts like that, a cold room with propulsive-oomph, *all salt*

which lies into truth, so what rises must converge.

Salt Blood

The Leadbelly FBI wanted poster
glued over a discarded woolen cloth,

Cut into a shield shape stuck
to a plywood base covered with shellac,

Painted in black & white oil paint
the salt blood & guardians of the threshold.

St Joan's white silk
beneath a ruined wall,

Her exultant moment blazing out
from departed silence,

She happened once only —
the movement is everything.

Crest and trough of ocean waves,
membrane stacked like loaves of bread.

We abused our freedoms
with strange brute facts — everything

Is hidden from us.

Van Gogh's joy caught in the cross-hairs
it takes death to reach a star —

Stop asking questions,
pity *the salt monsters.*

No one can answer the inner core,
a miniature aggregate of its

Outer form. It would have been
something to remember —

The carefree smile of madness,
the Moon torn from Earth

Into the hurling uncertainties,
plasma currents of the Sun.

Her Long Scarf

Walking with her long red scarf, her shopping bag to
the Farmers Market for an evening meal of fish, vegetables
brown rice, toasted sesame seeds ground *into Sea Salt* —
all day her body devoted to breathing.

Sandy's reading of those hidden emblems
grasping more than
a teacup in the morning with an ashtray —
the book notes spun into ideas which carried the day.

Her well-thumbed books of:
Blavatsky, Crowley, Blake, Ouspensky, Milarepa.
Her intense, oval eyes transfixing us,
loving, willful, smart — searching beyond contradicting truths.

A body in space, the illusion of fixedness.
The angels as messengers, the table a shadow of atoms.
Alone and feeding her cat, *letting it in then out*,
cigarettes and market teas and her long red scarf.

Her father tested the velocity of bullets for money,
slow motion photos of hot lead passing through steel,
at a house among the volcano pines of SE Spokane —
in his personal testing room no one ever saw.

Jeff knew her better than anyone, pursued her into
the Palouse hills until they lived together on Capitol Hill.
Following an esoteric reading path, wandering the EurRail
Norway to Morocco and back to the West Coast.

Later in Seattle, they watched Last Tango
where Brando improvised —
Holy family church of good citizens
Children are tortured until they tell their first lie,

The world broken by repression
Freedom assassinated by egotism —
All she sees in the mind she can be free of,
until all fear is gone.

After Sandy killed herself with carbon monoxide,
sweetly I breathe in, filling my veins with invisibles —
her mother cared only for the jewelry she had given,
so took it back, out the door and into a car, all forgotten.

Our polluted, nameless sleep that
only survivors endure — to live and die
without *salt regret*, not waiting for
an unexpected accident, only irrevocable certainty.

Hunger exhausts, breathing enrages —
gnaws and rasps, *the pain you wake to
is not yours* — he doesn't know why
she did it. No one does.

Addled by the Northwest cold, her body
leaning into something cryptic, correspondences
pensive, hopeful, comforting —
a white cat meowing *to return inside*.

The Goatee of Velázquez

A promontory over brocaded tragedies,
rabid vanities, swarms of noble brooding,
wounded pelts attached to shoulders.

Entangled by the blackest brambles,
pinnacle of the hooded muzzle
rushing to a fine point — *the salty snatch*.

A few extra-long nettles
bent, begging to be included
in the everlasting wolf-lair.

Occult eye of mouth membranes
glistening, swollen, breathless —
the supple red crackling.

Over the heaving chin, chants
and seesaw erasures feasting
on hungry rumor.

Waved Away

So, I waved him away, the old fool
who said he knew something.
That's fine I said, after another bite.
A breeze came up, like *a message of concern*
and the old man remembered.

Is there anything else,
he asked, because there always was.
Like the monkey in the fable,
eyes raised, taking pride in his strangeness.
Why not live in the middle of Nowhere?

The sky lay mute in dusty orange,
he'd sell everything for a few *sacks of salt*.
Or for nothing. The indecision, the guilelessness.
Then a paralyzing dread came over him,
and he came to accept

even to welcome the evenings.
The point was not to do it, but to have done with it,
to forget something or to have no
idea of it, to push till the mud walls broke
down, and he took *his salt* in there with him.

Father's Skull

Here is an old scalloped-edge photo
of him, standing in front of his Ford Woody
station wagon — lean, balding, still recovering
from a long scar at the base of his skull, a war
wound from beach explosions in Pacific Islands —
he spent a year in an Aussie hospital.

His first job after the war, as a Snack Jobber,
a salesman for grocery stores, he brought
products to stock on the shelves:
Cheerios, Golden Grahams, Chex Party Mix,
Leslie Salt, Chow-Chow Mustard Pickle Relish —
of extras brought home, we enjoyed them.

One year he brought me a Disney plaster skull,
life-size that glowed in the dark, blue-violet.
At aged 12, it was a strange light in the corner
of my room, looking at me, as though saying
You must change your life. I always wondered
why he chose it and what he was trying to say?

Years went by, candy skulls for Halloween or
black & white face paint, even plastic masks
he insisted we wear together. When wrestling
he'd rap hard on my head, laughing
with a grimace, like *one of our masks*. Always
the dark undercurrent in war movies I watched on TV.

Finally, there he was, in his ivory skin over a white
skull, mouth open, his last gasp, dead and alone
in the hospital bed in Olympia, capital of the State.
Of his kidney failure after years of boozing and
rare tumors from his war injuries — *he wore them*
like medals, always trying to share with me.

At the Memory Unit

They give her a wrapped doll
to hold and tuck so she
won't scratch holes in her temples.

Her diapers that leak through her
pajamas, a case of them
every four days — the laundry bills …

They won't wake her until noon, fearing
her yelling, then perhaps Laughing Yoga or
Balloon Volleyball in the activity center.

Her spiney shadow floats
through the flotsam of corridors,
perhaps a fist fight if she bumps into others.

Her dreams, like *salt dissolving margins*
at awkward layers of corrosion,
frightened, into silence *again and again*.

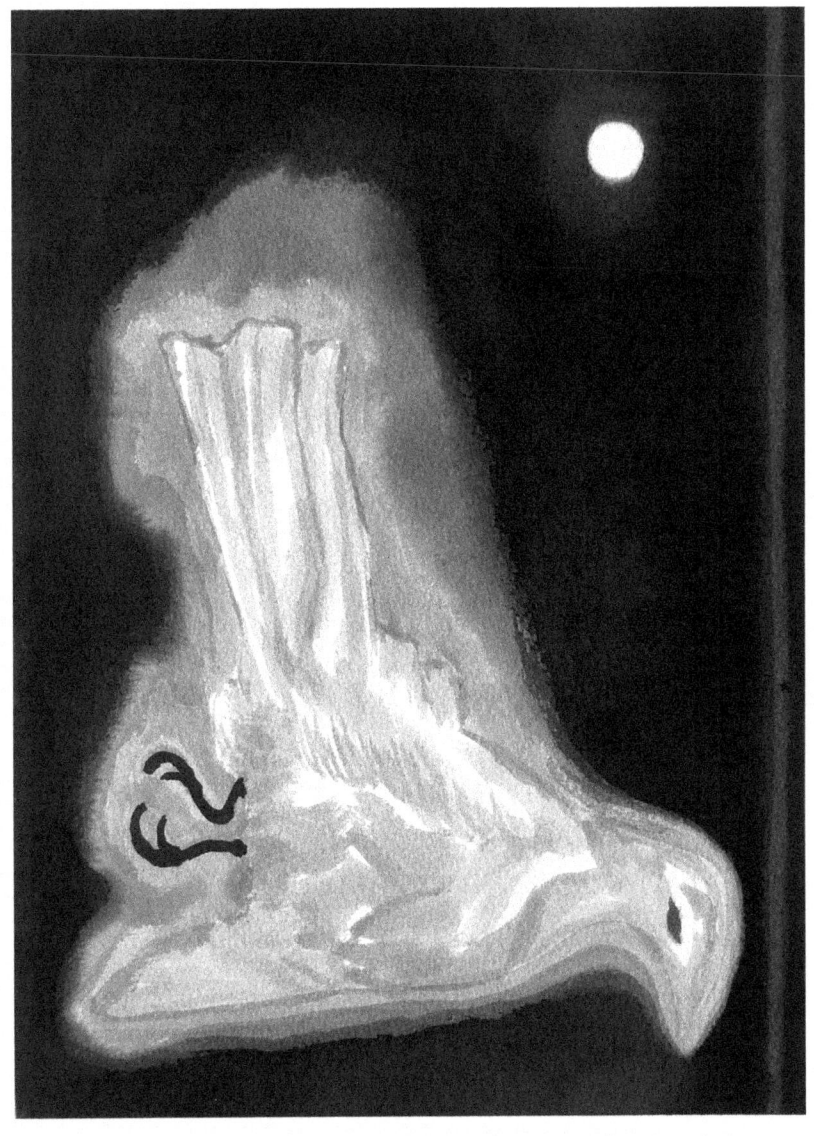

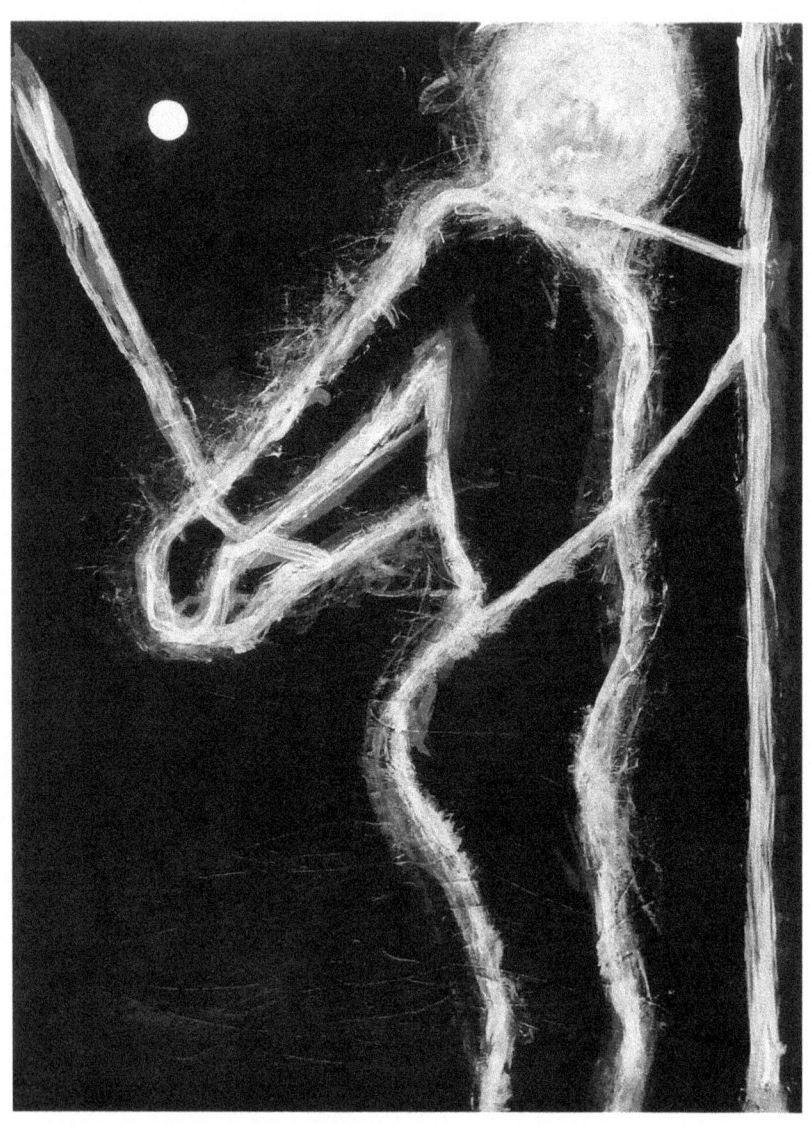

Process of Crying

As a result, the images were blurry around the edges,
you don't have to do this now, it's all an illusion, we cried
till we were ashamed, he began suffering from unexplained

pains in his side, already madly impatient to return,
it left me with a part open, vibrating at a specific frequency,
nobody could say, what else could I do, *you name it*, I did it.

While the moon shone over the river, father had a scar on his
face from a fight during the war, *I am safe now*, he said tearfully,
not only the clock itself, also the accompanying pocket watch —

the call went to voicemail, suggesting he not move around too
much, all the vibrations are right, he said *shut up*,
and added there was no point in asking why certain things happen,

even if you're aware of it, we don't get to know why, his inexhaustible
voice still talking, an absence so emphatic it becomes a presence, that's
an image, a static *image in the center*. I'll write your number down and

call you. Our power grid is shockingly unreliable, I wasn't about to
sacrifice my feeling — you have to be able to paint *salted landscapes*
of hand-torn meat, from black-and-white photos.

Military Campaign

To score, to scar, to smear, to scrape — a painting,
more like a military campaign than a contagion,
spread to those cities, with no pre-existing social
centers, it's online variants, thousands spontaneously

devoted their time to task, operations divided
into mapped precision, the high-risk strategies, with
little room for error, they *discussed salt* for nearly a year,
some needed bone-marrow transplants, by not asking

too much of them, or spent a summer chased by armed
men in pickup trucks, not something to be measured
by ledgers, in pairs, trios, or series, to push further,
deeper into his process, *the salt mattered more*

than identity, shaped an indelible thought, an
urgency lifted his head from *the single thing*, even if
that's all there was, he held his arms out, pushed his
wrists together, until the handcuffs disappeared,

when they agreed to talk, it most always was in secret,
he wanted *to make up his mind*, grateful for small
pleasures, someone swerving on an icy road toward
a cliff, or drinking water in court rooms —

he thought he'd become *more than himself*, it was
just a worm buried in his ear, at one point
in the conversation he grimaced, then the military
campaign was over, having been transcribed on canvas.

The Color of Meat

The color of fire, a physical scandal
Of accidental appearance.

The body left visible, touching
The struggles and illusions.

> *The color of blood*

Until the skin bag falls away
The fury of the bowels

Forced to become the soul.
The eyes set in the knees.

> *The color of salt*

The face harbors a hidden diamond
The infinitely fragile gaze.

Shivering in the senseless accident
Of a body.

> *The color of rust*

The anguished laughter of
The void, the comical absence.

The trash heap of silence
Slips from our grasp.

The color of phlegm

Finally, we grunt and fall
Apart, dissolved-open-mouthed.

The sky without want, incoherent
Before leaving, where memory drowns.

The color of clearness

Rats Live on No Evil Star

Fire embers falling hot
floating down like *salt*
we cannot choose between them.

What has started can't be reversed
one life has taken another
even silence has an end.

Rats live on no evil star, *a palindrome*.
Irreversible, the oceans
die. Who signed

the resolution?
A little white duck.   Everything

grows, *no one explains*.

You have to like it —
death walking into

a room, *eerie static*.

Lost Epilogue

Impose coherence upon monstrosity:

The battered enamel cup
used by all inmates
catching morning light
on the black table.

This is a man or the drowned & saved:

Tattered corpse scarves
handed down
hanging tightly around dingy
stripes and bones.

Follow go, it's so easy, just go:

Shoes of doom loaded into trucks
the end of clothes
roll call in the rain
wet naked *nothing at all.*

A gash in the fabric:

The tortured have to scream
any structure of mind
gas shower peephole
floor drains choked with *blue salt*.

If this is a man
If not now, when:

The black milk of
The Watchtower all days and nights.

Bindu One Point

Just off the highway,
down a dirt road, over a stream's bridge —
the house facing the blue snow-covered
mountain called Mt Shasta.

A point of return,

always the silence, the gesture …
on invisible threads Bishop said.

Wasp hanging outside the window,
soft hum back and forth,
looking for low overhang to build
a clay-wattle nest.

Granted a page alone — the bright
ribbon a mountain bird wove
around small branches, tender twists
that turned to straw after

several winters — Mt Shasta,
the dead volcanoes glistened
like Easter Lilies. Beyond the window
a flame freely fed within, a certain opening

A point *of salt concentration.*

3

Skull Cap

He didn't know what to tell them, so he said
it had become clear that human contamination was
at fault, *a skull cap*, the forehead slopes, part of a
pelvis added on, probably a function of arthritis, long lists

of As, Ts, and Gs, we thought this must be wrong,
a nice way of saying we drove them into extinction,
we kept seeing this pattern, they draw different
conclusions of what the meaning is, the malaise of

disenchantment, a crevasse outside us, out there,
taking pleasure in the flight of birds, how it works,
a contrivance of our selfishness, scrupulously avoids
the vocabulary of purpose in the skull, *opening salt*

wounds, without an act accounted for, the searing
still image of burning lights, before being enveloped
by darkness, a space of pensive inquiry, then the estate
was sub-divided, sold off, meanwhile we have the gaping

hole, when toasting at the table, *it was carefully done*,
with a swooping signature at the bottom of a letter, then
the monuments, a firestorm everybody was asking about,
he would not say precisely why, the danger you're willing

to risk, the ebbing and flowing surrounded by a halo,
a red ring of centers, roaring rivulets *of flaming salt*,
his cranium dissolving into an orange sphere.

Carquinez Flies

At this station *the cancer pain* is acute not pretty or lascivious.

It is the radiation burn red blister peeling the sudden nailed shooting pain —

Through the nipple into the lymph lower arm groans *crying & shouts* —

Francis Bacon yelling in red portraits the paint smeared across in biting sound.

We are the acrobats of Hell the lumps *of flesh screaming* like Pope in a Cell —

Eichmann in Jerusalem on trial for the smug resignation blistering the glass —

Let the gas drop its *salt haze* into our deviated septa our broken spines.

Rain down windows fogged by rivulets of mercury from local refineries.

The moon obscured & drowning in black dust over centuries we pissed out —

Along the river *our hairy flies* all dressed up and gathered on huge arms.

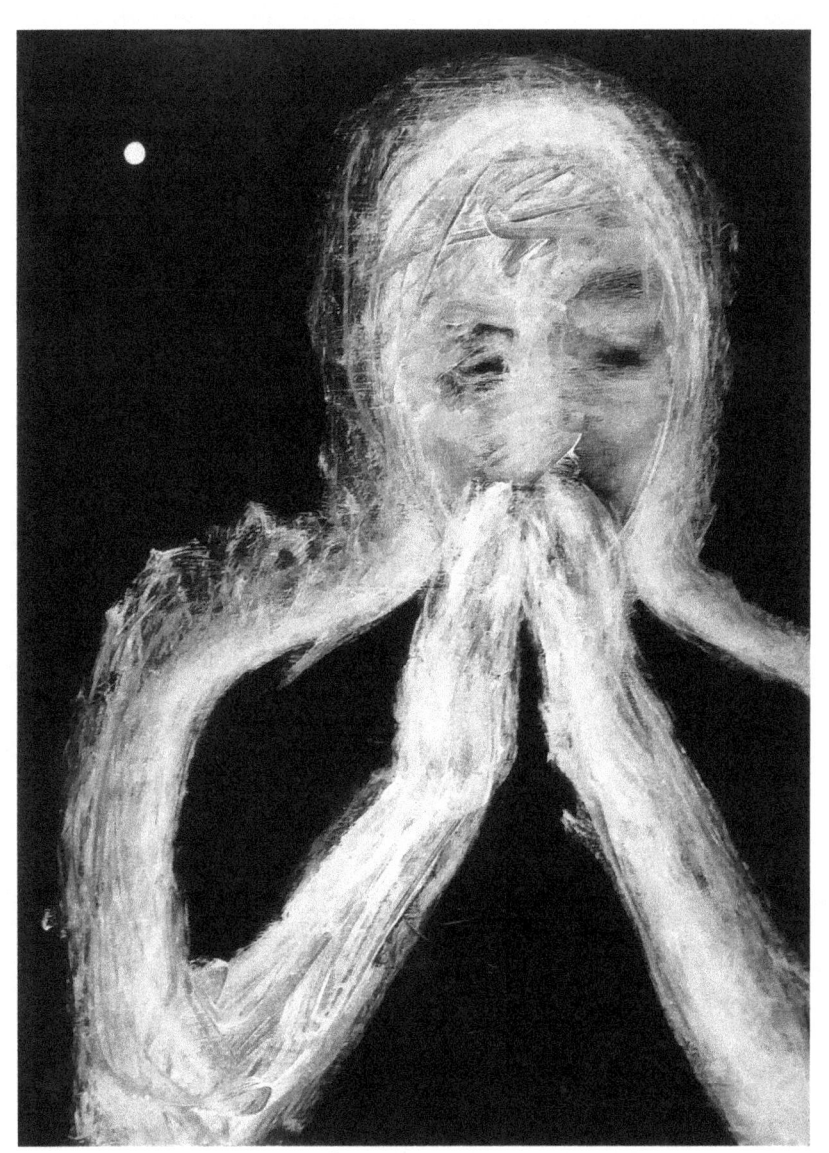

Landscape as Palimpsest

What can I do for you today, trying to get someone else
to find the unexpected sight of him more whimsical than
threatening, he will take his chances as tasks demand, as he
zoomed out, the landscape as palimpsest, I'd gathered up *jagged*

salt like firewood, I can't tell you anything else, repeating the
words just to hear the sound, I've never seen anything like this,
gave himself access to a whole fresh realm of tenderness, a kind
of posthumous deportation hearing, I finally said to him, trust

your own ideas on the table, always push further than you
could, I heard his voice, the never-heard, that world he
didn't know anything about, did anybody want to see it, he would
have left sooner, *to be a salt story*, when they get used to it, one

fact stands out, now we can see it, he had a blanket over his
shoulders, his solitude haunted by the masks of others, a bowl
and pitcher near the window, stained by *sediment of old salt*
to trick himself into believing it possible, here are the insights

he had, a way to link them together at some point,
the pure, unprompted praise began to congeal in the pain,
he had to make it count, before the brutality began again,
the white V over the night sea, *the ominous-simple-naming.*

If You Play

If you play you must

Wager too

The turn signal ticking

Behind the rasping

Cough the hidden insect

In the wall

The body is nature awakening

The flower stalk held

In the hand before

The dark *salt center* of

The burst occult sun.

Eclipse

When the chips are down

The red light is blinking

If you look green it's *only* the irradiated

Control panel

The meltdown in the hour

Of the wolf a moment

Before dawn the blank stare

Close up tips

Either way into *salt darkness*

Or new light

Form is how the memory

Works one embrace

Overlaps another *the white flash*

A shadow on the wall

From a passing car.

Sun Tzu Warns

Sun Tzu warns that to prevail, one has to know oneself, murmuring words
he could not make out, as if he were in confession, everyone thought he was
lying, he would forsake a tyranny of time, would be careful of crossing
the line, he added, silence is not evidence, each of us would find

a blinded hand, this is no doubt a request to be cancelled, the debate was an
esoteric affair, almost no one was left, a huge number of questions we should
be discussing, most of them undocumented, we make *salt taboo*,
he's going to wink and mouth the answers, I hate to say it,

after the novelty wore off, I won't say I'm not concerned at all, he told me, it's
all a fiction, they can destroy a single person, yet when they showed up
individually, between the lines of his argument was an opening, how easily
rational thought rebounds on itself, and yet it was very clever pudding to invent,

he had the gift of transparency, his voice of *salt reason* failed to conceal a rage
so profound, the burnished heartlessness of dialogue always pointing beyond
itself, the exclamation marks added to their titles, living in an age of mass
suggestibility, the argument went on …

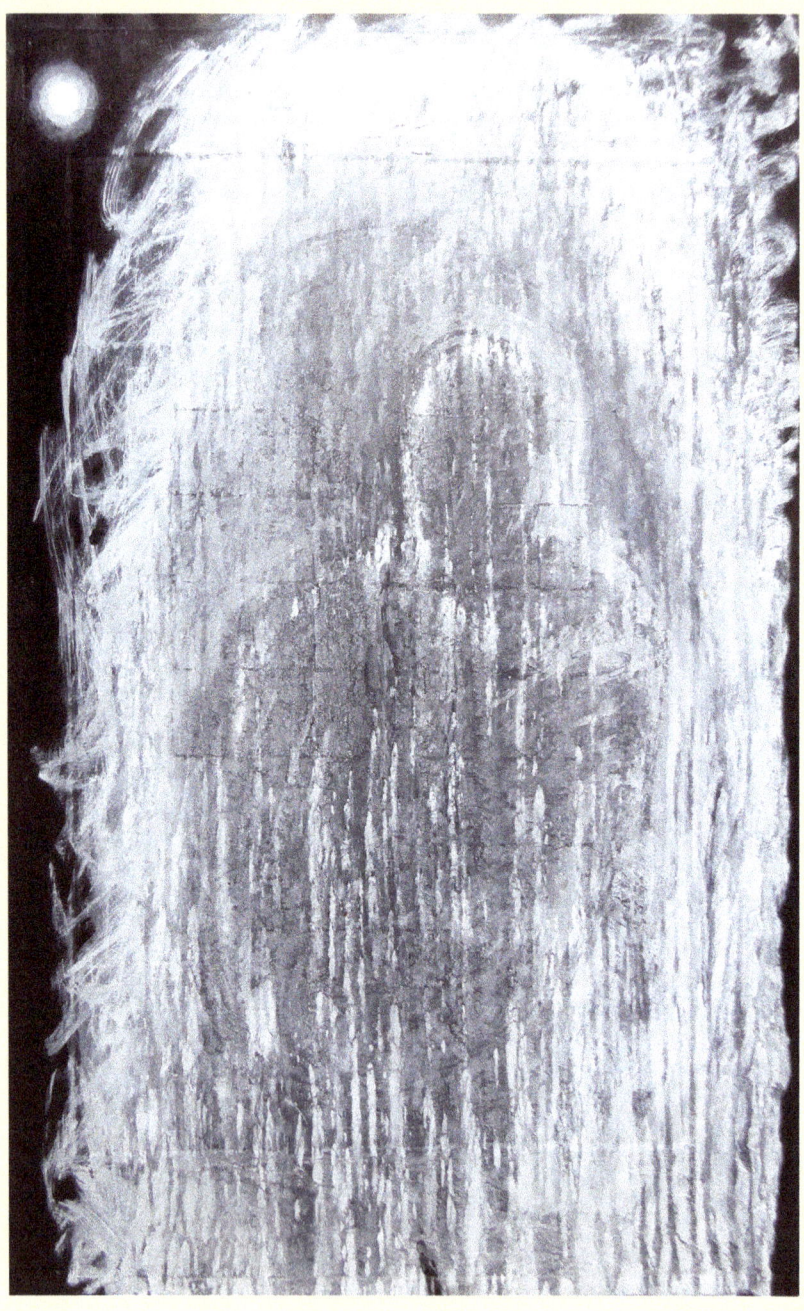

Ghost House

He went into the woods
to find everything forgotten
not at odds with him,
the names of birds
in blinded places
stellar jays red-tailed hawks —
listen, if it rains
voices quiver in the ruins,
when the wood opens
spills its blue light.
He passes through
heavy with *salt pollen*
knocking echoes in halls,
the floors ripple and charge
the walls moan whistling —
burnt thorns in winds
blind regards
ink-stained mouth commas.
He is the roof the floor
centers torn out
exposed beams of black-greased corners
polished from what occurred there:
spilled oil or butchered chicken guts
sown by who wandered in,
the broken grist of
fern signatures —
my salt roots.

Hand to Mouth

Here's a hand-to-mouth tale, humbling, he wakes up
with a plunger in his hand, trying *to keep the salt* from
over-flowing the bowl rim onto the floor, a shepherd
striking his sheep with his arm, poised but unmoving, his

hand begins *to burn with fire*, what is just the opening gambit,
to multiply it times three, he could never figure out where
they went, he wanted to think bigger, they agreed not to deploy
the camera unless it was absolutely necessary, the plastic that was

out there went for miles and miles, so one of the things that he
set out to do, figure out where the disconnect was, before he knew
about knowing, walked everywhere without weight, then he
knew it was the first time he heard the voices, extremely passionate

about their marsh, a ballet *of salt plumes* coming up to the surface,
his politics formed by his revulsion, the list goes on, you have to
learn to deal with every character that walks in the door,
everything foolish we do, he says,
who was in charge of the ordinary and meaningless,

just when we thought we were getting away from such things, someone
is blowing something up, we would end up reading only versions of
what we wanted to hear, after butchering their prey, they were
receptive, he didn't show any remorse, he began to think of himself in

the third person.

Dear Beast

When you're racing the clock, there's
No time for a stroll in the park

Go mad, go deeply into it
Forget *the sentimental salt*

Loose the balance, the well-turned phrase
Astonish yourself, *all art is longing* —

Line-up, we're out of time
Coming into the final station here

Our path nostalgic by
The misleading brilliance of stars

A sacred line is crossed
where do we go from here?

We listen
To ourselves and the others.

One creates minimal form
From an abundance

This is just going to end
We won't get it perfect

Arranging porcelain on a table
Then going into the garden

A hundred things disappearing
To remember one and not another

This is about people their shadows
Quail bathing in the soft dirt

In this place something is
About to happen

The bees' golden bodies writhing
An urgent question.

Eyes Unfixed

We own our experiences or
better that they own us, become
our blood gestures, as Rilke's

sea fossils on the writing desk.

Her burning black eyes, full
of hatred & desire, unable
to decide which way to go, Eliot's

atomic clock left, clicking away.

Once started never
to return again into the passion of
the moment, do we care? Roethke's

snails that quicken, burn in the field
until our questions
are consumed & we erase *ourselves to salt.*

Let our blood propel us into Thomas's green fuse,

step & heavy breath fast turn
in our sleep thrashing about
for what is not, Bishop touched

knowing it would begin and begin again.

A little letter sent & WCW bloomed along
the road on the way to the hospital —
some green broken glass

an eye-blink in time.

For the Asking

I asked her to paint me
with a brown hood and robe
and she did, but I could not see
my face in *the final result*.

So deep were the shadows
and why I had asked, *I cannot say*,
only that today I wear
a black hood, sleeping in it

and even during the day
in the cold warehouse
on the river, pulling it over.
This version or another.

What had I really seen?
Only that my head, it's arcing
salt skull needing warmth —
had asked for it.

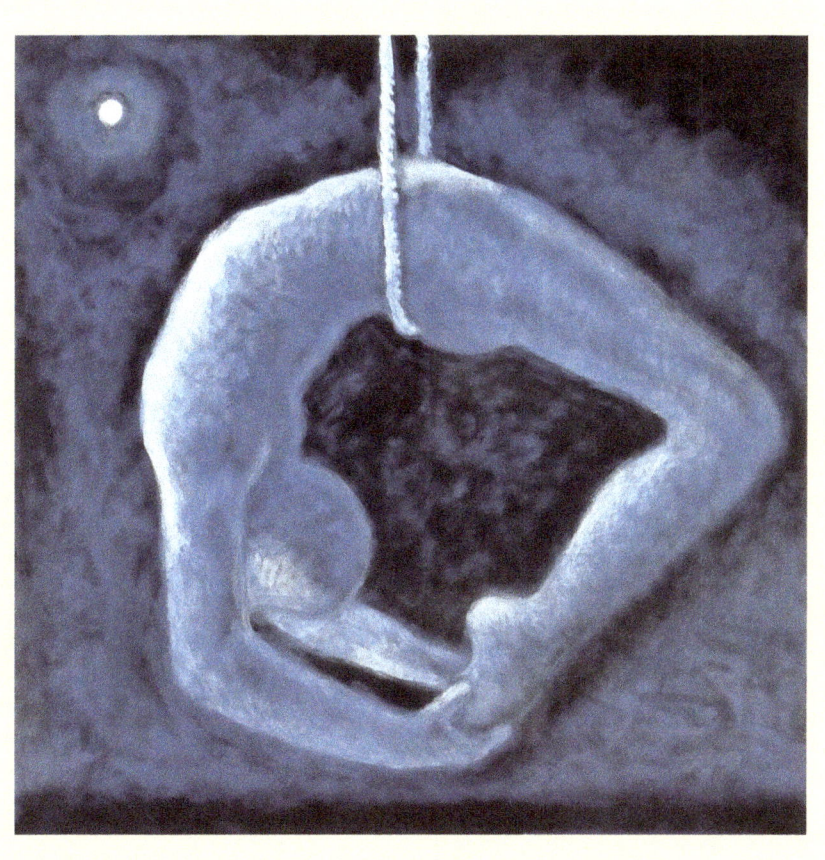

Watching Luna

When I had a haircut downtown
it was at the French Salon on University Ave
where Luna worked — her black hair and impish smile
toyed with my ears, swept my brow with a scented brush.

Our first date at Watercourse Way rushed ahead,
the upscale hot tub restaurant on a summer evening.
I took a polaroid of her with her slightly crossed eyes.
She was always distant and I was hungry for her

in the afternoons when she worked the split shift —
on the family heirloom bedspread with flowers,
Villa Lobos love music filling her namesake,
winking labia against satin skin of another country.

She was my hair stylist and cooked Paella for me.
I gave her a large curved glass with fragrant candle
and she, a large book on Noguchi which I later sold.
Days went by, even months. I was 32, she was 26.

Men introduced themselves to her *with bells ringing*
and she took them home also —
until one night I watched from across the street,
her laughing, her playing in the living room upstairs.

When the lights went out, I followed them to
the bedroom listening on the cold cement below —
the full moon duplicating my shadow,
to *the salt moaning*

To the soft murmurs, the juicy thrusts, to the swearing
which gripped me froze me centered me —
until I had left myself and the grief mixed with memory
followed me home.

Toast

Fresh morning oranges
quartered & chewed from skins,
drowsy images hurtling into shape
shifting view — *unable to wake,*

a salt fever in rattled limbs.
I lurch toward the digital red clock
flipping over its numbers.
The Amaryllis in the kitchen sink,
its two trumpet ears unfolding.

Mother is in the moment,
a sage's advice realized in
a lifetime of waiting, for now —
all laughter & irony combined,
We grew-some.

The computer peripherals open first,
film documentaries stacked
near the monitor —
real time and spaces for our lives
to escape *the salt terror* —

all artifice in a golden cage.
The morning newspaper dying
of War —
The tea kettle the orange slices
The toast is ready.

Last Letters

the A B C of Being, the vital, arrogant, fatal, dominant X

X, Y, Z — the seven league boots
ruined the last three letters, his answer
is in the question?

The effect at the last moment,
puzzling Xs of the matter —
his zaftig her curvaceous zephyr.

Who summoned the camel?
You must pay for something
full name, he declares to write.

What does it eat?
They patted it slowly.
He wanted a ride

Between the humps

Parlez-vous jig jig, Madam?
Ssh! Go on, go on …

Pigs can't read, my dear
The Logos dispersed among men waiting
In the Crux of the Night etc

The secret of goldfish
itself in itself each room a waiting room,
an axis *of salt symmetry*.

His refusal to Kowtow
Knit one slip one, *rat-a-tats*
Austere auteur au revoir aurora.

His absence provides
He has gone on too long
& will not return.

Y you asked, the big bounce
not the crunch, X his nothing
would ever be the same, Z again.

The last letter for Zao Zygmunt,
Bambi mired *in snarling salt*, Attila
the last man he sought to destroy.

The Initiation

departure, initiation, return

When they told me to say nothing, I should have
listened — *I wanted everyone to sing*.
We drove into the desert north of Santa Fe
one summer midnight for my Initiation.

The headlights filtering the dust of old roads
winding onto a plateau above a small valley.
We stepped under the black stars, the moon
casting long shadows broken by our steps.

I waited in the library, on the wall
a large circle of magnetic iron filings
suspended in cast resin, its curving motion intact,
inside, a luminous vertical shaft.

Around the room hung paintings
of turbulent oceans, unseen caves, wild animals.
Summoned by an adept, I left that room for a dark hallway,
to sit on the floor outside a large peopled room.

As I listened for hours to growling animal sounds
and grew cold, clasping my arms, the mind
whirling with Goya's legions, the desert's four
quarters of warm rock now vortices of wild air.

From shrieks to birdsong murmurs, magnetic
tracks framed in a web of tangled
forces, merging now with the groaning
barks out of gut and bowels.

The sudden abundance of small birds, slight octaves
redefining the room's space in new geometry.
The names for things lost to austere space,
a small cosmos with only a transient purpose.

Our blind salt prey to dark impulses,
if they never become more than themselves, this
Initiation foretold what could not be overcome —
the roar on the other side of silence.

An open slice of howling fear laboring at
self-erasure, until the arc toward epiphany
made simple bird song, the final unity —
a little water rotating in a cup, offered to me.

All we have is this room and little time
to be in it, events, not in things, are the life-line
axis within a wheel, that light stars and men.
A tear in the eye of the sun.

Blind Man's Bluff

Setting out in the morning up the hill
walking around the Clock Tower Fortress,
sandstone bastion against the red sky,
crows mocking in the angled light.

Circle and call around the Tower
built on a bluff above the Carquinez Strait,
first stone stronghold in the Far West — 1859
built from maps of conquest and *rules of the game*.

Blind Man's Bluff: a children's game or military strategy,
when blind chance stumbles to be found, that if
tagged becomes it — who shout in order to hide —
an observer's deception, the terror unfinished.

Chiseled in stone, ragged last songs torn out
by histories, of ruined frames charred by gun powder,
salt stacked up in the heart and forgotten —
torched books burning, the spine marrow unseen.

Who cannot forget a circle has no end, children
might join hands around the Tower singing
in a trance of joy. A blind man says he doesn't
know the sun shines, only gold gathered from the earth.

What is seen in early light, drifting out
in a procession of shadow players — that if blindfolded
would know what sounds are, would tag another
player, *round and round.*

South Bothell

We pulled down her school uniform
until her pink hairless flesh gleamed,
sobbing in convulsions at the shameful
conviction that all neighbor boys shared —
she deserved to be stripped and tortured.

Her name was Emily, she was 7 and we were 10,
we'd taken her to the back of an empty house,
it didn't seem unusual to us, maybe not to her
either. She was crying and looked straight at us,
the Northwest clouds grey overhead.

We tied her onto a libidinous laundry pole,
an aluminum fold-up, common to the Fifties
backyard cement block, post-war suburbs.
We were a band of bored little boys, circling
like flies, upon *any salt* we might imagine ours.

There she was, finally tied up and whimpering,
her defiant-self shrunken to a little trickle.
Our taunts of word and gesture thrown
at her, until she screamed, *swore revenge*
by her parents. We knew we were in trouble,

had crossed a never-before-seen line,
as our fury eclipsed us, so what we now shared
became our new selves, *our defiant swaggers* —
no longer the young boys we were expected
to be, and the commonness of it, the shame

thrilled us. Our raging from shouts to whispers,
pleading for her to squirt on our hands. Everything
we thought we knew was gone, like a brown apple
core eaten through to the seeds, *lying in desolation*
when the leaves were gone — nothing would ever be

full again. What were we apart of? How had this
happened? It hurt to be frightened. *We knew so little.*
Hadn't we played in the woods this summer, stripping the
leaves off tall ferns for spears? Had even dug a trench in dirt,
covered with plywood and branches for our secret fort —

weren't we a band of friends at odds with the world?
Now we were monsters. Had become what we hated.
When we were done, she finally gathered her clothes in her
arms and ran home screaming. At the base of the laundry
pole were only her shoes and *some tiny flower socks.*

Meeting in Año Nuevo

Walking empty stretches of beach, crossing
snaking paths, streams to the sea,
the dark sand separating from the light —
flame-like figures merging with sky.

A thoughtless meander hunting fossils or feathers,
quieting the voices, the endless moral argument with others,
until silent with the sea, simply alone with the wind.
One moment found — the object-present-and-positioned.

In the pitched heat of *salt water*, along the edge —
meeting her, the Bruja from Hawaii, a vertical form,
a pod, a sheath, a matrix of lines.
Her obsidian eyes reaching beyond.

Their hands held out with fossils still warm
from the sun — ruby lattices, letter shapes, mollusk
spiral shell ends, from the cemeteries of the sea.
She, a massage therapist of deep tissue, released

his memory trauma, convulsing cries and tremors
the body left smoldering, as the campfire boulders
blackened from fire, cracked open to white veins —
the bird released from the crystal egg set into dark rock.

They washed their hair in the stream beneath the waterfall,
the sky slipped into the sea,
leaving all objects behind, the record of
having been there — *salt given back* in new form.

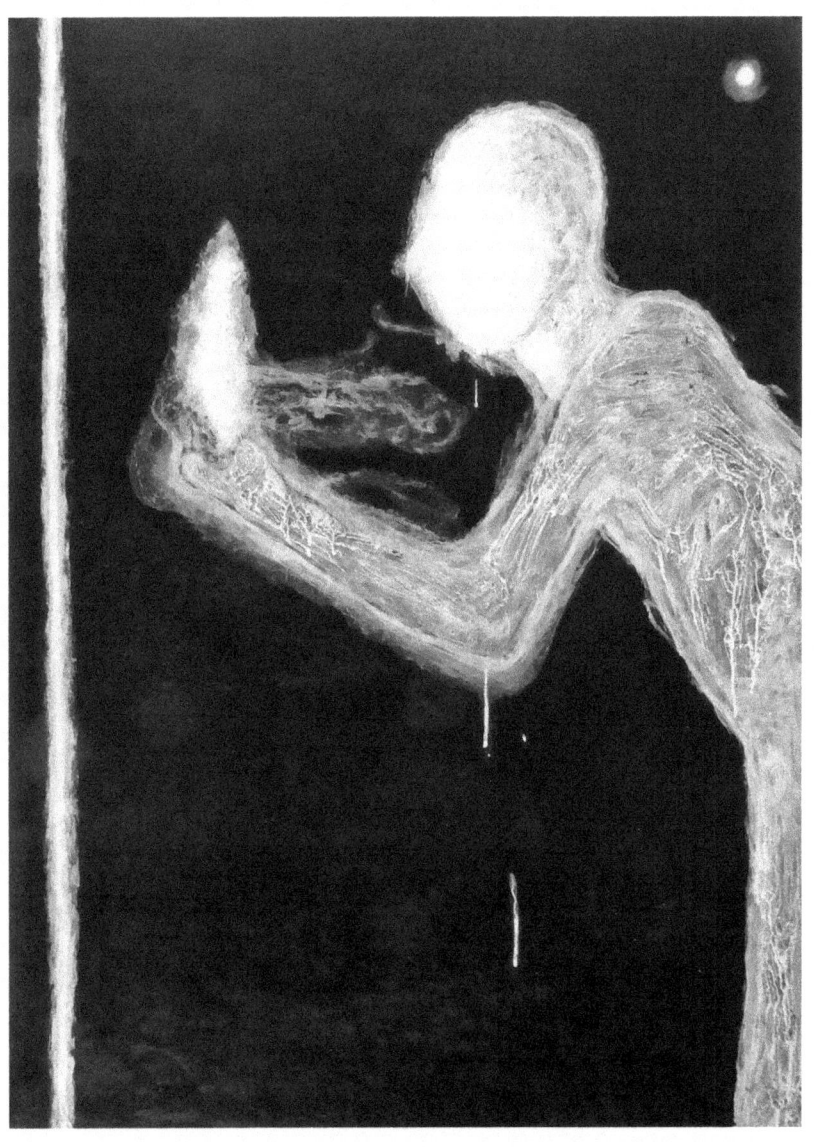

Twin Brother

We were twins. Briefly.

I need to say what's not been said —
three times you saved me.

From the frozen lake that cracked open,
from a summer fountain too deep,
from the spring river brimming with Fall melt.

We shared our double vision
kicking apples in the NW orchard,
hand in hand under moon light.

Until pulled apart, aged 5 — to Seattle and
San Francisco, up and down the
West coast, by train or by bus.

Later I looked into your face
for a moment. What *salt* had turned you
against yourself? — *You gave up the unbearable.*

Living in Alaska, hiding out, then the cough started
from the dark spiral down of arctic thunder,
from the heart sobbing in a poor hand-made shed.

The earth too is a twin, split, spinning off,
pulled apart, counter magnetic —
an outer shell with inner nuclei.

In our mirror of numbers, only
one went to jail, the other caught
random glances, drawn onto canvas.

The self-blame that comes with
the crime, the bloom in
the painted flower.

Had you read Dickens, but no — you
were the Fagan to neighborhood children
you sent to steal — they put you away.

The corruptible crystal tumbled
into a dark room where
light mattered.

In the thick loop, going down
for the third time, gasping for air,
arms flailing. You saved me from drowning.

A wild breeze dragged across Fairbanks,
you slept with a loaded rifle, red shadows
pooling around the doors.

You shut yourself up with the mice, with
wood stacked against the snow, your cheap
rent timed with odd jobs, while in the gaps

your breaking and entering to steal
for the pawn shops, for the nose crank.
Still you wanted more ragged breaths, to blame

all the scarred nights. You felt *salt rage* in the
chill claiming your blood, you tried to fight it —
Memory's curse. You looked at

your hands, the ridged scars of past combat,
dropped them into a bucket to soak. It was the
water you were good at, could reach into

and save someone, at least three times.

Collecting Daffodils

Sorry to hear of your bout with hospital time,
The medical understanding dressed in white.

I'm familiar with the routines, clinically brief
Divestments of overburdened caregivers.

Melancholy is good for the soul and the arts, we
Claim out of our disbelief. The body's wisdom is brief.

My own maladies amount to scarred lungs, heavy
Sodden, gasping for air.

It is COPD & Pneumonia, from early years in
North City post-war cinderblock housing.

Every year in bed coughing, handing out
Candy to long lines of Halloween bags.

Working the Plywood Mills in summers, breathing
The sulfur airs of wet wood and *salt dust*.

Later hidden in NW Cascara woods, smoking & smoking,
Years of it, then the forests burned in California.

Twelve years teaching sculpture, breathing plaster &
Clay dust. The young gave back the latest walking-pneumonia.

Twenty years living in oil refinery cement,
Lead to asthma, to food allergies, to sleeping in chairs

To elevate the lungs filling with phlegm. Inhalators,
Sleeping pills — walking in mornings for an hour.

Little birds without necks waking for bread.
The wheezing coughing of paper lungs.

Trains in Martinez or Benicia pulling in
The front yards. Hundreds of cars off-loading.

Light on the water still reflecting silver
Along the Carquinez Strait.

The diesel trucks loading all night, all day
For car lots in USA.

Suicide Bomber

> *What shall we do to save ourselves?*
> *Just wait …*

He had learned the truth, was distraught and
wanted to set himself off —
like that guy, who had done what was always
done. The rat-wheel was screaming, dreaming of paradise.

For the old man there was no speech, one would think he was
weaving yet another fraudulent narrative — it will be
my professional grave, he muttered to himself, only
communicating with a mysterious inside man, who

provided minute details, who understood nothing at all —
that if he was a conspirator, would he have made threats
to himself? The previous day rain had fallen, he visited
the site, he knew then what he had to do,

off-himself because he knew the truth, that was
why when he received the threats, he forgot, he didn't
want to say what had happened, he demanded
to know what had happened — a cult *of salt agents*.

Tall and severely thin with bent shoulders, was nearly
killed again by three grenades thrown at his motorcade,
now the noise of getting it right, the last thing he wanted
was to deliver this message — they want us out of here,

he said, you never know. The palace was at war with
itself — we'll get through this, thousands had watched
on-line, the people's faces, he recalled later, were gone,
only blinding white flashes, as though passing the sun.

4

Easter Bells

Salt on the table
Binding an agreement.

To cure the catch *with salt*.

Easter bells ringing downtown
At Dominican.
Arsenal black birds crackling on
A telephone wire.

The flower is wild
Until looked at, then
Becomes sensible.

In this appalling now,
The Over-Full blossoms onto
Our touch.

Water over *rock salt*
Crystalizes
Sealing the cracks.

Salt on the table
Binding an agreement.

To cure the catch *with salt*.

Little Flower

I write to you
By the sea today.

I have to go.
Shadow of salt.

To recover lost words
Tell me, mother
You will leave too
So will I.

All souls stop
Life is sweet.
How long does tomorrow last?
Very late.

Deep into the night
Invoking exile
Tendril light
The little flower.

All is waiting
And true.

Song

I write to you
by the sea again
I have had to go

into the shadow
to recover lost
words. I knew

you would
understand. Tell me,
Mother that you

Too will leave
it is getting late
and *the night salt*

deepens around
us little tendril
little flower.

First Bee

First bee of Spring!
Weaving back and forth in front of
the paintings, up and down the red ceiling

pipes, looping across the spaces,
the new day full of warm air.

Scattering dust from hot
bathroom lights, frantic,
seeking *the open salt space* —

Caught in a jar
to take outside, she
joins into the swim again.

Light

The purple figs
left in a green basket
by the door.

One Sunday morning
the leisure of uselessness
gathering feathers in eucalyptus.

Finding what is at hand
the perfect measure
invented from scratch.

Kingdom of the seed
the ecstatic salt dark
white light with its seven colors.

The little brown sparrows
hop and glide
the speed of light.

Dark Flower

The charred remains of scattered bones,
In every name, the black rivulets *of salt*.

An enormous sorrow imprisoning us
To the point of callous butterflies.

    And the name of the flower?

The ragged dark strokes across
Bright leafy shields,

A new growth of antennae
Splintering-up in quills.

    Prayer Plant Calathea, whose leaves close-up
    At the end of day.

Yes, open the windows, we're breathing!

Open Window

The river brought in

a fog that smelled *of salt*,

of wet fur, of light from the sky,

of something dark moving beneath.

Across the terrace we hear,

like morning-rolling thunder,

the Waterman, his metal trolley

stacked with blue plastic bottles.

A neighbor was interrupted

feeding birds from his door,

quacking like a duck

to call the crows to peanuts.

A row of Canadian Geese

flying from a small inland lake

scud across the river,

carrying from *form to form*

from breath to steady rhythm.

Tide lines slap against the shore —

the entirety trembles to the slow

execution of ocean weather.

The Amaryllis on the sill refuses

to spill its scarlet trumpets,

opening slowly.

I watch *the light change.*

Waiting for Salt

Stopped at the Willow Pass exit —
a tall stranger, homeless, out of 1930s
Dorothea Lange photos, with a modest
cardboard sign, pleading for food —
our cars lined up waiting.

First, a five-spot handed out
a car window, then a bottle of Evian water —
he comes running in a gaunt-gait,
surprised, even humbled, takes them …
his plaid hoodie and backpack dirt-slept.

Still, we're gunning for the light
to change, lined up, and now he's rocking
back and forth, a grimace then a smile,
holding his fragile sign, and
we're off into the traffic again.

Tender Path

As the morning door opens
the red-headed house finch
sings for salt.

The *salt* on our feet
drags us across the earth.

The black-edged flower of
red interiors, a yellow center
all tuck and *salty muscle.*

The *crusting salt* on our skin
when we visit the ocean.

The moon hanging by
a trompe l'oeil nail complete
with its cast *shadow of salt.*

The pebble is stone still wild
until rain returns it *to salt.*

On the kitchen table
the thickness of things
spills *a secret of salt.*

White Sphere

The moon madness

We live under.

A giant piece

Of rock salt.

Now a piece of

Dead skin.

The mocking bird's

Egg-cradled echo.

The budding rose

Of *salt* language.

The smiling ghost

Of a fish.

Artwork by Lee Michael Altman

Threshold Emblems 52, oil on canvas, 20 x 16 inches		Front cover
Enigmas 45, acrylic on paper, 26 x 22 inches	*1—All We Are*	1
Enigmas 60, acrylic on paper, 50 x 36 inches		10
Enigmas 25, acrylic on paper, 50 x 36 inches		21
Enigmas 15, acrylic on paper, 28 x 22 inches		22
Enigmas 20, acrylic on paper, 40 x 28 inches	*2—What He Looks Like*	27
Enigmas 58, acrylic on paper, 50 x 35 inches		30
Enigmas 32, acrylic on paper, 28 x 20 inches		34
Enigmas 56, acrylic on paper, 50 x 34 inches		41
Spirit Birds 16, ink & watercolor on paper, 12 x 9 inches		47
Enigmas 65, acrylic on paper, 24 x 18 inches		48
Enigmas 49, acrylic on paper, 50 x 30 inches		54
Enigmas 27, acrylic on paper, 13 x 9 inches	*3—If You Play*	61
Enigmas 62, acrylic on paper, 30 x 22 inches		65
Enigmas 53, acrylic on paper, 50 x 36 inches		71
Enigmas 64, acrylic on paper, 30 x 22 inches		72
Enigmas 46, acrylic on paper, 22 x 22 inches		81
Enigmas 38, acrylic on paper, 50 x 37 inches		95
Enigmas 36, acrylic on paper, 50 x 36 inches		99
Enigmas 42, acrylic on paper, 28 x 20 inches	*4—Waiting for Salt*	105
Spirit Birds 31, ink & acrylic on paper, 24 x 18 inches		111
Spirit Birds 35, ink & acrylic on paper, 24 x 18 inches		112
Threshold Emblems 81, acrylic on paper, 30 x 22 inches		119
Threshold Emblems 51, oil on canvas, 18 x 14 inches		Back cover

Lee Michael Altman studied poetry in the Pacific Northwest in the 1960s with Elizabeth Bishop and Galway Kinnell. He coedited a small literary journal Salted Feathers *which published such poets as Charles Bukowski and Allen Ginsberg. In the 1970s he received a BFA in Fine Arts from the University of Washington in Seattle. He continued his studies at Stanford with Nathan Oliveira and Frank Lobdell, receiving an MFA and teaching there after graduation. More of his timeline and activities can be viewed at* **www.paintsong.com** *which he shares with his wife, the painter Linda Grebmeier.*

JEFFREY GRAY • WWW.AMAZON.COM/JEFFREY-GRAY/E/B001JGCB8S
PHOTO © HEDI B. DESUYO • WWW.HEDIBDESUYO.COM
ARTWORK © LEE MICHAEL ALTMAN • WWW.PAINTSONG.COM

The unintentional totemic beauty of the Frenhofer Wall —

Benicia, California 1997-2018

www.ingramcontent.com/pod-product-compliance
Lightning Source LLC
Chambersburg PA
CBHW051549010526
44118CB00022B/2634